EAR TRAINING FOR PRACTICAL EXAMINATIONS

MELODY PLAYBACK/SINGBACK 1

A COMPLETE COURSE OF EAR TESTS
FOR PRACTICAL EXAMINATIONS

BY

BORIS BERLIN and ANDREW MARKOW

<u>Part One: Levels (Grades) 1 to 4</u>
Part Two: Levels (Grades) 5 and 6
Part Three: Levels (Grades) 7 and 8
Part Four: Levels (Grades) 9 to 11 (Associateship)

ISBN 0-88797-262-4

Copyright 1986 The Frederick Harris Music Co., Limited
Oakville, Ontario, Canada

Printed in Canada

INTRODUCTION

The purpose of this set of books is to provide a series of practical playback (singback) tests for both teachers and students. These tests meet the requirements of most examination systems, particularly those of the Royal Conservatory of Music, the Western Ontario Conservatory of Music, the Western Board and others. They are invaluable as the basis of a sound preparation for examinations and auditions and offer a wealth of material to be used in furthering a comprehensive musical development as well as in assessing current progress.

Since these tests are universal, students are advised to cover them thoroughly for their own over-all musical development and enrichment regardless of whether or not they take examinations.

The playback (singback) tests in these books cover all levels (grades) from one to eleven (Associateship) and, as in the case of the lower levels, comprise all the possible combinations as required for examinations. In general the tests consist of an extensive number of aural playbacks (singbacks) to be used in the musical development of all instrumentalists and vocalists and as such should be both sung back and played back on the respective instruments.

Groups of tests are designated by A, B and/or C. Tests designated by A correspond to the current requirements of the Royal Conservatory of Music, those by B to the requirements of the Western Ontario Conservatory of Music, and those by C to the requirements of the Western Board. Nevertheless, we strongly recommend that the current syllabus of each examining board be consulted for its respective requirements in each grade.

Boris Berlin
Andrew Markow

HOW TO USE THE BOOK

The intent of these tests is to help the student prepare for the playback (singback) section of the ear test part of practical examinations as well as to develop musical memory, a sense of observation, aural recognition, playing by ear, an awareness of note patterns and shapes, a feeling for intervallic relationships, and a keen perception of melodic and rhythmic design.

For best results the student should cover at least one test DAILY by (1.) naming its key; (2.) playing the tonic triad; (3.) playing the test twice while observing the DIRECTION of the notes, the PATTERNS they form and the over-all shape of the melody; (4.) singing or humming it back; and (5.) trying to play the melody back from memory. If necessary each step can be repeated until (5.) is attainable.

The teacher will explain and illustrate how the melody is structured, i.e., the way the notes move by step or by skip (intervals) to form patterns, scales, broken triads or chords, repeated notes, etc. The student's attention must also be drawn to changes in direction (up or down), the over-all design (shape) of the melody and the feeling of the rhythmic pattern.*

At the lesson the teacher should check the student's home practice by using the examination procedure: choose one of the tests, name the key and play the tonic triad, and then play the melody twice, asking the student to sing (intone or whistle) and play back the melody. A parent, brother or sister, or a friend can also assist by giving tests using the same procedure.

By commencing at a lower level the student will develop his or her skills progressively. Regardless of the level used, however, the student should start at the beginning of the level in order to achieve a good understanding and a solid foundation.

---

*See the set of books on rhythm in this series, Rhythm Clapback/Singback 1-3.

LEVEL 1 (GRADE 1)

A

Four-note melodies based on the first THREE notes of a major scale and beginning on ANY of the three notes. Keys of C, G or F major.

DIRECTIONS:
  Name the key.
  Play the tonic triad.
  Play the melody twice observing the DIRECTION of the notes and the PATTERN they form.
  Finally, SING or HUM the melody without looking at the music and then PLAY it back from memory.

Key of C major.   Melodies with notes moving by *step* and with *repeated* notes.

Key of G major.   Melodies with notes moving by *step* and with *repeated* notes.

LEVEL 1 (GRADE 1) continued

Key of F major.   Melodies with notes moving by *step* and with *repeated* notes.

Mixed keys.   Melodies with notes moving by *step*, with *repeated* notes and with a *skip* (interval) of a third.

LEVEL 1 (GRADE 1) continued

LEVEL 1 (GRADE 1) continued

LEVEL 1 (GRADE 1) continued

A

LEVEL 2 (GRADE 2)

Five-note melodies based on the first FIVE notes of a major scale, beginning on the TONIC (1st) or DOMINANT (5th) and in the keys of C, G or F major. The melodies may contain one or more skips (intervals) of a third and/or repeated notes.

DIRECTIONS:

Name the key.
Play the tonic triad.
Play the melody twice observing the DIRECTION of the notes and the PATTERN they form.
Finally, SING or HUM the melody without looking at the music and then PLAY it back from memory.

Mixed keys. Melodies with notes moving by *step* and beginning on the *tonic* (1st) or *dominant* (5th).

1

2

3

4

5

6

7

8

Key of C major. Melodies containing one or more *skips* (intervals) of a *third*.

9
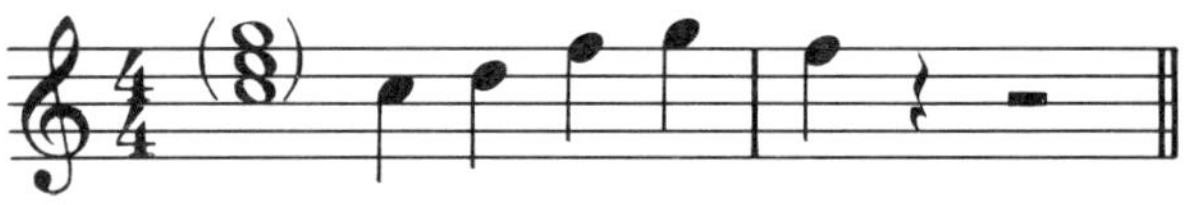

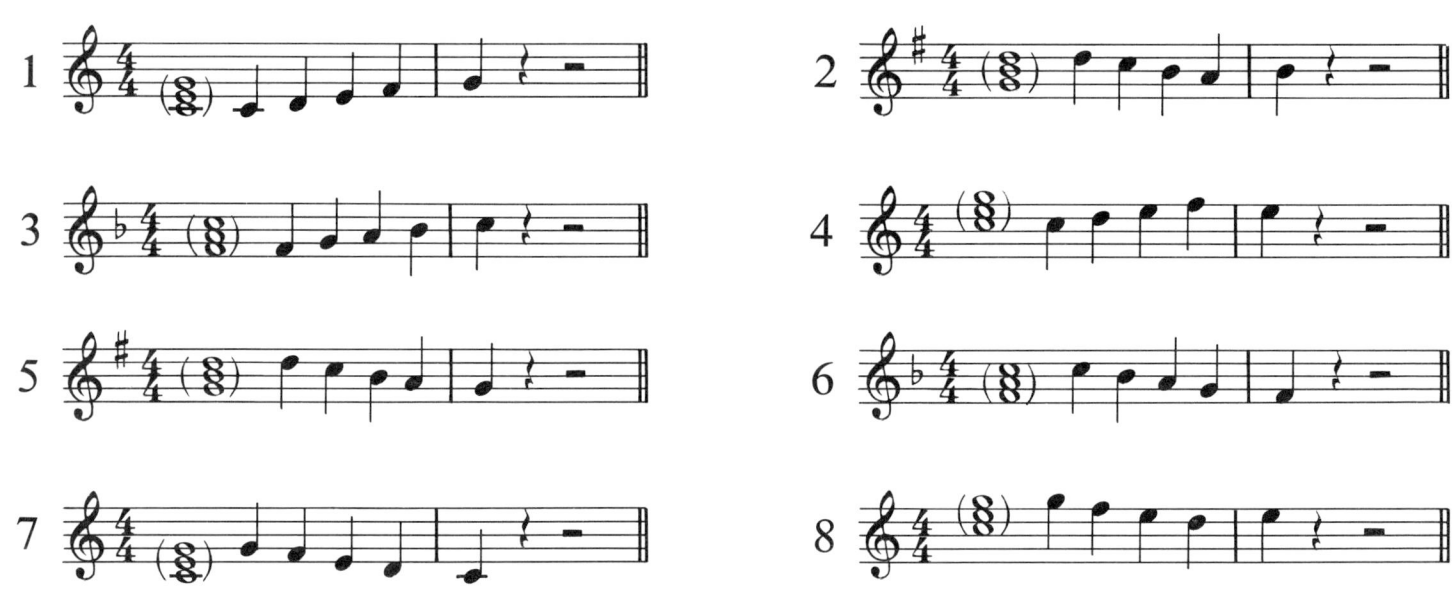

10
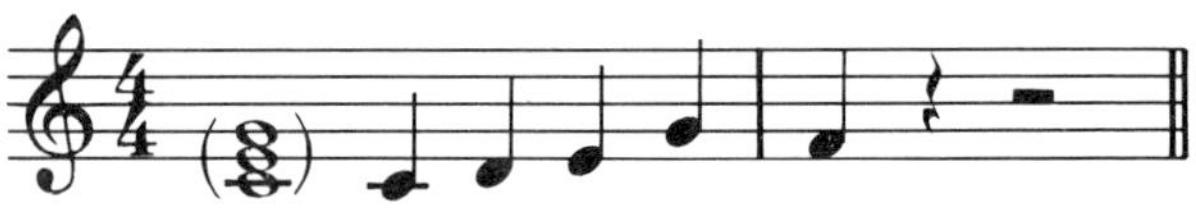

11
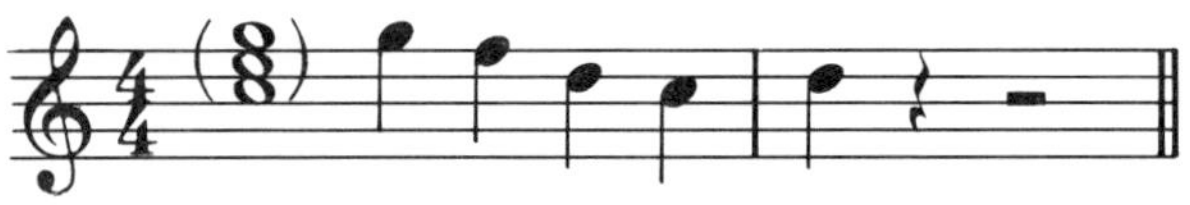

12
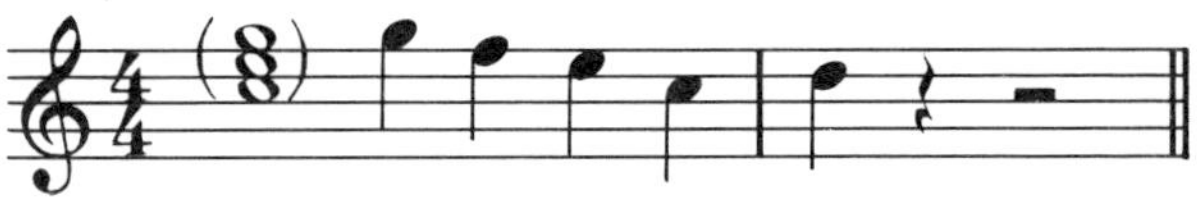

13
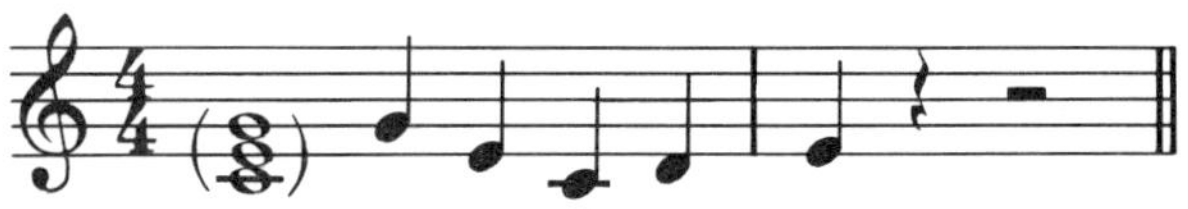

14
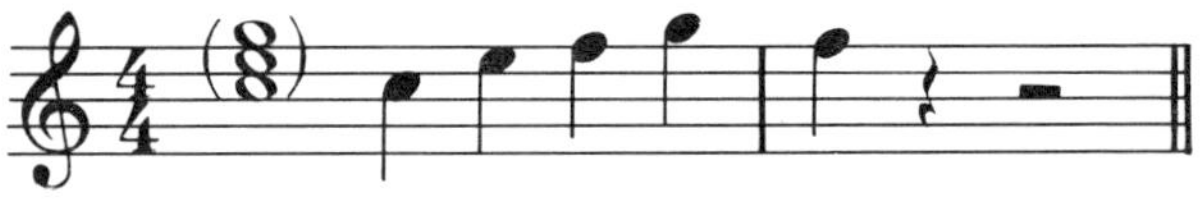

15
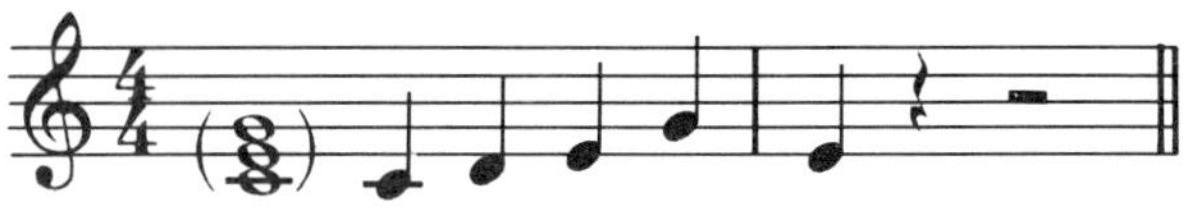

16
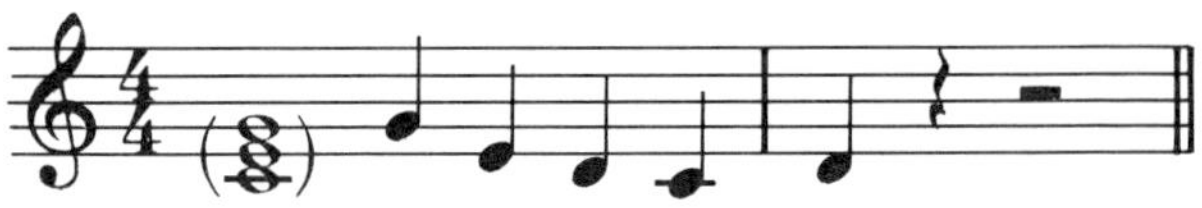

17
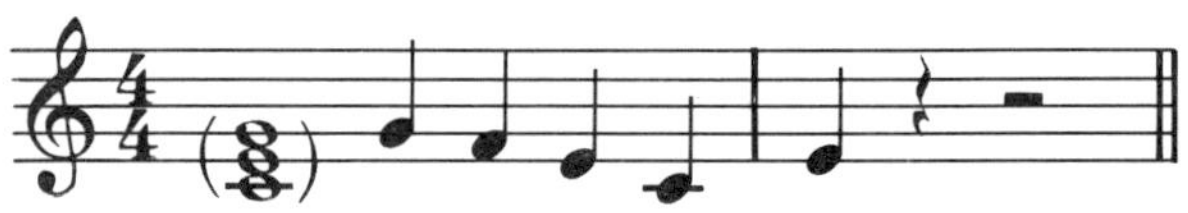

18
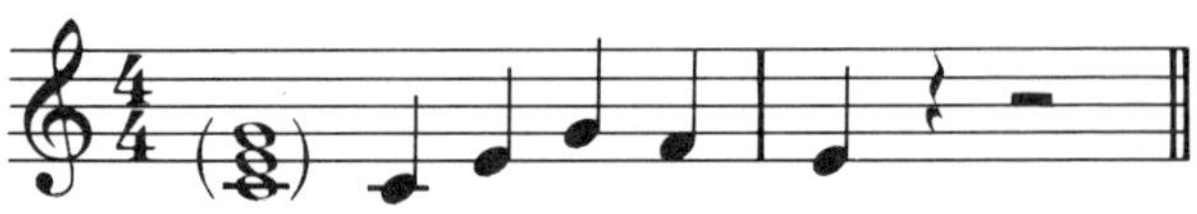

19
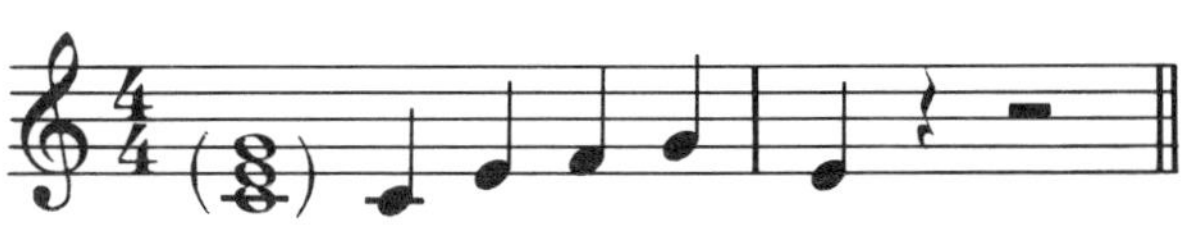

20
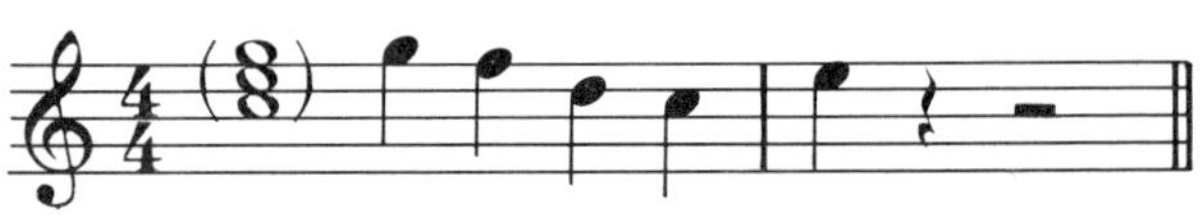

LEVEL 2 (GRADE 2) continued

Key of G major.   Melodies containing one or more *skips* (intervals) of a *third*.

Key of F major.   Melodies containing one or more *skips* (intervals) of a *third*.

LEVEL 2 (GRADE 2) continued

Mixed keys. Melodies with notes moving by *step*, with one or more *skips* of a *third* and/or containing *repeated* notes.

LEVEL 2 (GRADE 2) continued

LEVEL 2 (GRADE 2) continued

LEVEL 3 (GRADE 3)

Five-note melodies based on the first FIVE notes of a major scale, beginning on the TONIC (1st) or MEDIANT (3rd) and in the keys of C, F, G or D major. The melodies may contain one or more skips (intervals) of a third and/or fifth and repeated notes.

DIRECTIONS:
Name the key.
Play the tonic triad.
Play the melody twice observing the DIRECTION of the notes and the PATTERN they form.
Finally, SING or HUM the melody without looking at the music and then PLAY it back from memory.

Mixed keys.   Melodies with *skips* (intervals) of a *third* and beginning on the *tonic* (1st).

Mixed keys.   Melodies with *skips* (intervals) of a *third* and beginning on the *mediant* (3rd).

LEVEL 3 (GRADE 3) continued

Mixed keys.   Melodies with *skips* (intervals) of a *fifth* and beginning on the *tonic* (1st).

Mixed keys.   Melodies with *skips* (intervals) of a *fifth* and beginning on the *mediant* (3rd).

LEVEL 3 (GRADE 3) continued

Mixed keys. Melodies with *skips* (intervals) of a *third* and/or *fifth* and with *repeated* notes, beginning on the *tonic* (1st) OR *mediant* (3rd).

LEVEL 3 (GRADE 3) continued

LEVEL 3 (GRADE 3) continued

18

A B

LEVEL 4 (GRADE 4)

Six-note melodies based on the first FIVE notes of a major scale, beginning on the TONIC (1st), MEDIANT (3rd) or DOMINANT (5th) and in the keys of C, F, G or D major. The melodies may contain one or more skips (intervals) of a third, fourth and/or fifth and repeated notes.

DIRECTIONS:
Name the key.
Play the tonic triad.
Play the melody twice observing the DIRECTION of the notes and the PATTERN they form.
Finally, SING or HUM the melody without looking at the music and then PLAY it back from memory.

Mixed keys.   Melodies beginning on the *tonic* (1st).

Mixed keys.   Melodies beginning on the *mediant* (3rd).

LEVEL 4 (GRADE 4) continued

LEVEL 4 (GRADE 4) continued

LEVEL 4 (GRADE 4) continued

A B

In addition to the 80 previous tests, the following melodies contain SEVEN notes.

B

In addition to the 90 previous tests, the following melodies contain EIGHT notes.

LEVEL 4 (GRADE 4) continued